Contents

Gone forever! 4

Sabretooth's land 6

The tar pits 8

Plants 10

Living with the Sabretooth 12

What was the Sabretooth? 14

Growing up 16

Learning to hunt 18

Sabre teeth 20

Sabre attack! 22

Sabretooth's prey 24

Dire Wolves 26

Where did the Sabretooth live? 28

When did the Sabretooth live? 29

Fact file 30

How to say it 30

Glossary 31

Find out more 32

Index 32

Some words are shown in bold, **like this**.
You can find out what they mean by looking in the Glossary.

Gone forever!

About 25,000 years ago, many giant animals lived around the world. Most of these animals are now **extinct**. This means that they have died out. Scientists find out about them by studying their **fossils** dug out of rocks.

One of these extinct animals was the Sabretooth. The Sabretooth was a large cat that hunted other animals. It was named 'Sabretooth' because of its long, sharp teeth. These were shaped like **sabres**, a type of curved sword.

Sabretooth's land

Once there were pools of sticky **tar** in California, in North America. Plant seeds and animals became trapped in the tar. The seeds and the animals' bones show scientists what the area was like when the Sabretooth lived.

The **valley** of the **tar pits** was dry and warm. Grasses covered the ground and there were only a few trees. In summer the weather could get very hot. Even in winter the weather was not very cold.

7

The tar pits

Many bones of the Sabretooth and other animals have been found in the **tar pits**. The **tar** was often covered with water. Creatures that came to drink got caught in the tar and were unable to escape.

This is a model of a trapped mammoth at the La Brea tarpits in North America.

Sabretooths sometimes tried to eat the animals stuck in the tar. Often, they got stuck in the tar, too. Their bones were added to the thousands already caught.

Plants

The seeds and leaves **preserved** in the **tar pits** tell scientists which plants grew at the time of the Sabretooth. Scientists also study the numbers of each type of seed. This tells them which plants were most common.

a fossil of a seed

Grasses were the most common type of plant at the time of the Sabretooth. There were also some trees. Animals that ate grasses and animals that ate trees have been found in the tar pits.

Living with the Sabretooth

The **fossil** bones of other animals have been found in the **tar pits**. Some of these bones belonged to an animal called the **Ground Sloth**. They tell us what the Ground Sloth was like when it was alive.

The Ground Sloth was a big, powerful animal.
It weighed about as much as two cars and was
nearly 3 metres long. The Ground Sloth had
huge claws on its front feet and it ate grass
and other plants.

What was the Sabretooth?

Many skeletons of the Sabretooth have been found in the **tar pits** and in other places. The bones show us what the Sabretooth looked like. They show that the Sabretooth was a type of cat about 2 metres long.

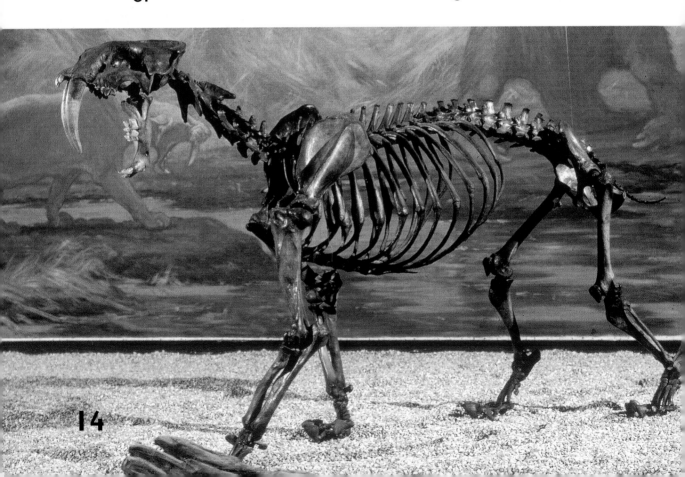

The Sabretooth was a very strong animal. It had powerful front legs and paws with sharp claws. The Sabretooth was probably not a very fast runner. It crept up on its **prey** and killed it with its teeth and claws.

Growing up

Scientists think that baby Sabretooths were like lion and tiger cubs today. They did not have the same long teeth as the adults. They could not defend themselves from other hunting animals. They may have hidden in long grass.

This is a modern lion cub.

Baby Sabretooths were probably protected by the adults. Several females may have lived together. One would look after the young while the others hunted. The young would have spent lots of time playing with each other.

Learning to hunt

As a young Sabretooth got bigger it grew long teeth and strong muscles. By the age of six months the young Sabretooth was almost an adult. It began to hunt its own food.

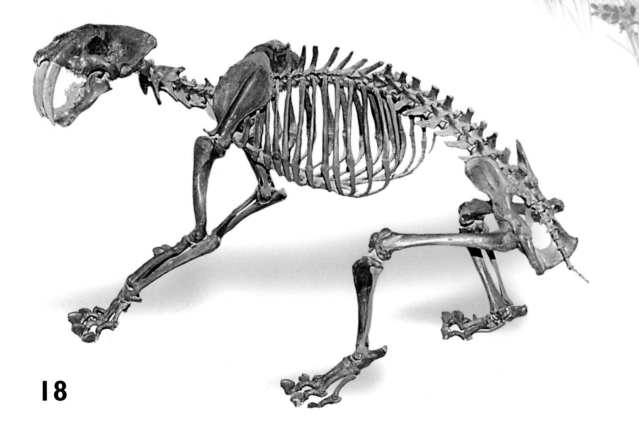

At first, the young Sabretooths went hunting with their mothers. The adults taught the young how to move silently and how to hide in tall grass. This was how Sabretooths crept up on their **prey**.

Sabre teeth

The Sabretooth is named after the long teeth in its upper jaw. These teeth had sharp points. The teeth were **serrated** (jagged) like a knife along the back edge. The Sabretooth also had very strong muscles in its neck and shoulders.

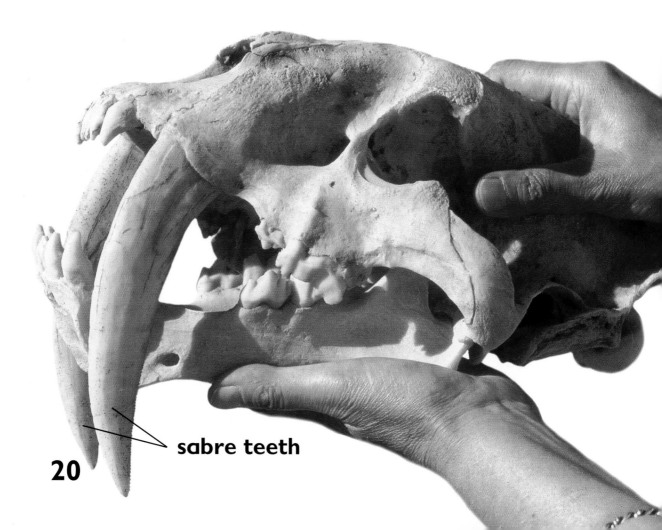

sabre teeth

20

The Sabretooth used its long teeth to kill its **prey**. The cat knocked its victim to the ground and held it down with its front legs. Then the long teeth were stabbed into the neck to kill the animal.

Sabre attack!

The back legs of the Sabretooth were short and strong. The bones show that these legs had very powerful muscles. The Sabretooth used its back legs to leap forward quickly.

The Sabretooth crept as close as it could to its
prey. Then it dashed forward at top speed.
The Sabretooth tried to catch its victim before
it could start running away.

Sabretooth's prey

The bones of the Sabretooth's **prey** have been found in the **tar pits**. These show that the Sabretooth hunted large plant-eating animals. The Imperial **Mammoth** was one animal that Sabretooths ate. They also ate horses and **bison**.

an Imperial Mammoth skeleton

horses

bison

The Sabretooth preferred to hunt large animals. One successful hunt would provide plenty of meat. But mammoths were big and strong. The Sabretooth probably only attacked mammoths that had got stuck in the **tar**.

25

Dire Wolves

Other hunting animals lived at the same time as the Sabretooth. One of these was the **Dire Wolf**. The Dire Wolf was a large animal like a dog. It may have hunted its **prey** by chasing it for long distances.

Sometimes Dire Wolves tried to steal a meal from Sabretooths. Dire Wolves were smaller than Sabretooths. But if there were enough Dire Wolves they could join together to drive Sabretooths away from their food. Then the Dire Wolves would feed.

Where did the Sabretooth live?

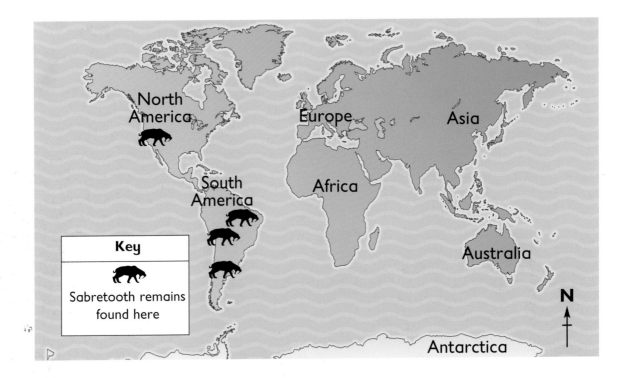

The Sabretooth lived in North and South America. Open grassland covered the land. The Sabretooth roamed across this grassland. Different kinds of sabretoothed cats lived in other parts of the world.

When did the Sabretooth live?

The Sabretooth lived between about 1 million years ago (mya) and 15,000 years ago. This means it lived in what scientists call the Ice Age.

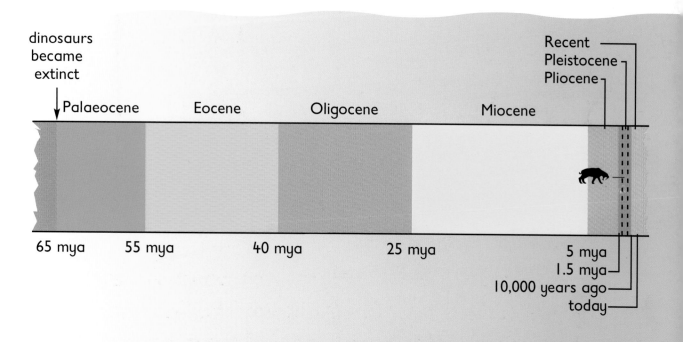

dinosaurs became extinct

Palaeocene   Eocene   Oligocene   Miocene

Recent
Pleistocene
Pliocene

65 mya   55 mya   40 mya   25 mya   5 mya
1.5 mya
10,000 years ago
today

Fact file

Sabretooth fact file	
Length:	2.2 metres
Weight:	400 kilograms
Time:	Pleistocene, about 1 million to 15,000 years ago
Place:	North and South America

How to say it

mammoth – mamm-uth
sabre – say-bur

Glossary

bison plant-eating mammal, like a large hairy cow

Dire Wolf type of wolf that was larger and stronger than modern wolves

extinct an animal is extinct when there are none left alive

fossil remains of a plant or animal, usually found in rocks. Sometimes the remains have been turned into rock. Most fossils are bones or teeth because these hard parts are more easily preserved. Some fossils are traces of animals, such as their footprints.

Ground Sloth plant-eating animal. It lived in North and South America at the same time as Sabretooth.

mammoth type of elephant that lived at the same time as Sabretooth. A different sort of mammoth lived in cold parts of the world. It had a thick fur coat and is called the Woolly Mammoth.

preserve make something last a long time

prey animal which is hunted by meat-eating animals

sabre type of long, curved sword once used by soldiers

serrated blade with many tiny zig-zags along its length. The cutting edge of a steak knife is serrated.

tar black, sticky liquid. Tar bubbles up from the ground in some places.

tar pit place where tar comes to the surface from deep underground

valley low area of land found between hills and mountains

Find out more

Here are some books on Sabretooths:
Ice Age Sabretooth, Barbara Hehner (Crown Publishers, 2002)
Prehistoric Mammals Colouring Book, Jan Sovak (Dover Publications, 1991)
The Mammals, Hugh Westrup (Millbrook Press, 1996)

Look on these websites for more information:
www.enchantedlearning.com/subjects/dinos
www.enchantedlearning.com/subjects/mammals

Index

claws 13, 15
female Sabretooths 17
fossils 4, 10, 12
grassland 7, 11, 19, 28
hunting 15, 18–19, 23, 24, 25, 26
legs 15, 22
muscles 18, 20, 22
other animals 8, 12–13, 24–5, 26–7

plants 6, 10, 11
size and weight 14, 30
tar pits 6, 7, 8, 9, 10, 12, 14, 24, 25
teeth 5, 15, 18, 20, 21
weather 7
young Sabretooths 16–19